Faith, Love, and Patience

A GUIDE TO

2 THESSALONIANS

Faith, Love, and Patience

A GUIDE TO
2 THESSALONIANS

SUSIE SHELLENBERGER

NELSON IMPACT
A Division of Thomas Nelson Publishers
Since 1798

www.thomasnelson.com

Published by Nelson Impact, a Division of Thomas Nelson, Inc., P.O. Box 141000, Nashville, Tennessee, 37214.

Scripture quotations noted NCV are from the New Century Version®. Copyright © 1987, 1988, 1991 by Word Publishing, a Division of Thomas Nelson, Inc. Used by permission. All rights reserved.

Scripture quotations noted NIV are from the New International Version. Copyright © 1973, 1978, 1984, International Bible Society. Used by permission of Zondervan Bible Publishers.

Scripture quotations noted TLB are from *The Living Bible*, copyright © 1971 by Tyndale House Publishers, Wheaton, Ill. Used by permission.

ISBN: 1-4185-0540-4

Printed in the United States of America.

05 06 07 08 09 RRD 9 8 7 6 5 4 3 2 1

Contents

Introduction:
First Things First

"HEY, JANNA." MONICA SMILED AS HER FRIEND SLID INTO THE BOOTH ACROSS from her. "What's going on?"

"I'm really glad to see you right now."

"What's up? Are you okay?"

"Monica, I'm just feeling so guilty! I did some things before I became a Christian that I'm not proud of, and I can't stop feeling guilty."

"Well, have you asked God's forgiveness?"

"Yes," Janna said. "And I know God has forgiven me. But every now and then Satan brings the past to my mind, and I start thinking I've blown it way too much to ever have a real future with Christ. I mean, I want to know beyond all doubt that I'm going to spend eternity with the Lord."

"You *can* know that, Janna! The Spirit of God living inside you is far greater than Satan. Don't let him fool you."

"See, that *sounds* good, but how do I actually make it happen? I feel so hopeless. I keep wondering if I've already missed out on what God has in store for me."

HAVE YOU EVER FELT LIKE JANNA? HAVE YOU CAUGHT YOURSELF WONDERING IF somehow you're missing out on all that God has in store for you?

Well, you're holding the right book at the right time! The apostle Paul gives great insight, teaching, and answers through his second letter to the Thessalonians. The Thessalonian people had some of the same questions you have. As you soar through the pages of this study, you'll learn how to apply 2 Thessalonians to your life with relevancy!

And the cool part? There's no pressure to hurry up and finish this study in a specific time frame. In fact, it's broken down into small chunks—called "Scoops"—so you can easily do a little at a time. Think of this book as a multilayered ice-cream cone. You wouldn't want to eat the entire thing at once. Simply enjoy a little at a time . . . scoop by scoop.

2 THESSALONIANS

❊ **Where is it?** In the New Testament. After 1 Thessalonians and right before 1 Timothy.

❊ **Who wrote it?** The apostle Paul wrote 2 Thessalonians approximately one year after he wrote 1 Thessalonians.

❊ **Why should you be interested?** The Christians to whom Paul wrote were confused. Have you ever doubted your faith? Have you experienced spiritually confusing days? Then you'll relate to this book!

❊ **To whom was this letter written?** The church in Thessalonica. These people were fairly new in their faith. They'd been Christians for almost four years. In our study of 1 Thessalonians, we learned that Paul, Silas, and Timothy were persecuted for their faith and run out of the city of Thessalonica.

The Christians to whom Paul was writing were also being persecuted for their faith and thought they were experiencing the Great Tribulation. They were saddened and dismayed because they thought they had missed the Rapture.

One reason Paul wrote this second letter was to clear up the confusion and to teach them that the Rapture and the Great Tribulation had not yet occurred. How did Paul know that? The Bible describes specific events that must happen before the Rapture and before the Great Tribulation, and these events had not yet occurred.

❊ **One more thing:** If you've ever felt as though you have no future, you're totally, way-out, absolutely *wrong*. And this second letter from Paul to the Thessalonians will prove it. You not only *have* a future, but God desires for your future with Him to be filled with vibrancy, hope, and expectancy. Sound good? I thought so. Dig in!

CHAPTER 1

Not Enough to Believe

From Paul, Silas, and Timothy. To the church in Thessalonica in God our Father and the Lord Jesus Christ.

—2 Thessalonians 1:1 NCV

Which specific church do you attend?

Are you a member of this church?

List as many Christian denominations as you can:

Sometimes Christians become more concerned about the name of their church than the One the church serves. In Paul's greeting, he reminds us that all Christians are part of a much bigger Church than one that meets in a building. As Christians, we're all part of the most important Church of all—the body of the Lord Jesus Christ.

Grace and peace to you from God the Father and the Lord Jesus Christ.
—2 Thessalonians 1:2 NCV

Define *grace*:

Grace can mean:

___ a. You get excused from geometry class.

___ b. You get to eat dessert before dinner.

___ c. You're excused from the punishment you deserve.

___ d. You're really smart.

Check this out: "For all have sinned and fall short of the glory of God" (Romans 3:23 NIV).

Who has sinned?

Now grab your Bible and look at Romans 6:23 (NIV). What are the wages of sin?

We could paraphrase this verse by saying:

___ a. The wages of sin is eternal homework.

___ b. The price of lying is death.

___ c. It costs too much to go to heaven.

___ d. The price tag on sin (or the cost of sin) is death.

Let's look at Romans 3:23 again and keep going through verse 26. According to these verses, what can we place our hope in even though we've sinned?

As sinners, we deserve the death penalty. But God is so crazy about you —so in love with you—that He sent His only Son, Jesus Christ, to pay the death penalty for you, to save you from your sins.

Though we deserve to die, God offers us grace through His Son. We are justified by His grace. That means when you come to Christ and genuinely repent of your sins, He not only forgives you, but He justifies you: He looks at you *as if you've never sinned*!

Paul began his greeting to the Christians with grace and peace. We can't experience God's peace until we've experienced His grace. If you've repented of your sins, accepted Christ's forgiveness, and are walking in obedience to Him, you're able to experience His deep peace.

But you can't have His peace until you first seek His grace.

If you've never asked for God's grace, you can do that right now by praying the special and life-changing prayer below.

STOP & PRAY

Dear Jesus: I believe You died on a cross so that You could pay the death penalty for my sins. I don't deserve that kind of love. There's no way I'll ever be able to pay back that kind of debt. But Jesus, I accept Your death, Your forgiveness, and Your grace as a gift. Thank You so much!

Will You forgive my sins? I'm so sorry I've broken Your heart and done things against Your will. I want to live for You. I give You my entire life right now. I want You to be in charge. I'm not going to sit in the driver's seat of my life any longer. I choose to give You that role. You lead, and I'll follow.

Thank You so much, Jesus, for dying for me, for resurrecting Yourself from the dead, and for preparing a place for me in heaven right now so that someday I'll get to live forever with You. As I grow stronger in my relationship with You, saturate me with Your blessed peace.

In Your name I pray these things, amen.

● _____ **SCOOP 2** _____ ●

Let's look at 2 Thessalonians 1:2 again: "Grace and peace to you from God the Father and the Lord Jesus Christ" (NCV).

Paul's gentle spirit shines clearly in this greeting. He's writing to Christians who are confused and discouraged. So instead of reprimanding their immature faith, he encourages them by giving a blessing of peace and reminding them of God's grace in their lives.

When you're confused or discouraged, what do you do (circle all that apply)?

CALL A FRIEND   Drink a soda   Go to bed   *Pray*

Cry   *Write in a journal*   Watch TV   **SCREAM**

Talk to Mom or Dad   Run   Bake cookies   Sing

Talk with a sibling   *Laugh*   Read the Bible

SURF THE INTERNET   LISTEN TO MUSIC   Swim

Grab your Bible and read John 14:27. When you're confused, what does God want to give you?

According to this Scripture, what two things does Jesus encourage us *not* to do?

1. _____

2. _____

We must always thank God for you, brothers and sisters. This is only right, because your faith is growing more and more, and the love that every one of you has for each other is increasing.

—2 THESSALONIANS 1:3 NCV

If you'll flip back to Paul's first letter to the Thessalonians, you'll notice that he commends the Christians for their faith, love, and hope. Now, in his second letter to the Thessalonians, he commends only their growing faith and their love. What's missing?

The Thessalonian Christians were confused. They thought they had missed the second coming of Christ; therefore, they lost hope. Grab your Bible and turn to 1 Corinthians 13:13. What are the three things that Paul says will continue forever?

1. _____

2. _____

3. _____

And what is the greatest of those three?

Though love is greater than faith and hope, all three elements are necessary for Christians because without faith and hope, we can't truly experience love.

Paul encouraged his friends by reminding them that he was praying for them and thanking God for them. How does it make you feel when someone tells you he or she is praying for you?

Whom in your life can you pray for and encourage?

1. _____

2. _____

3. _____

4. _____

STOP & PRAY ————————————————————

Close your devotional time by praying for each of your family members.

SCOOP 3

So we brag about you to the other churches of God. We tell them about the way you continue to be strong and have faith even though you are being treated badly and are suffering many troubles.

—*2 Thessalonians 1:4 NCV*

As Paul was writing this letter, Christians were being ganged up on, beaten, and run out of their homes. Paul was saying, "We're proud of you Christians! You're enduring tough times. God is with you!"

All Christians will experience some tribulation. If people are giving you a hard time for your faith, you can actually rejoice because you must be doing something right! That means people can see God in your life.

Grab your Bible and flip to 2 Corinthians 4:8–9. According to this passage we are experiencing some things, but we're not experiencing others. Fill in the blanks:

(Verse 8)

    We have _____,
        but we are not _____.
        We do not know _____,
        but we do not _____.

(Verse 9)

        We are _____,
        but God does not _____.
        We are _____,
        but we are not _____.

This is proof that God is right in his judgment. He wants you to be counted worthy of his kingdom for which you are suffering.
                    —2 THESSALONIANS 1:5 NCV

Though we'd all love to avoid trouble, as Christians we should learn to expect to be hassled because of our faith. Check this out: "So do not be ashamed to tell people about our Lord Jesus, and do not be ashamed of me, in prison for the Lord. But suffer with me for the Good News" (2 Timothy 1:8 NCV).

What does Paul ask us to join him in?

Describe a time when you were made fun of because of your faith:

Though we may be hassled because of our faith, we should always remember our Christian brothers and sisters in other countries who are facing harsh persecution—being jailed, forced into slavery, being separated from their families, and even killed.

Take a moment right now to write a prayer for Christians who are in the midst of persecution:

God will do what is right. He will give trouble to those who trouble you. And he will give rest to you who are troubled and to us also when the Lord Jesus appears with burning fire from heaven with his powerful angels.
—2 THESSALONIANS 1:6–7 NCV

God *is* just! You never have to worry about settling the score, because you can count on Him to do it! It may not be in your timing, but God will settle the score. God is a righteous judge. Grab your Bible and turn to Romans 9:14. What question about God does Paul ask in this verse?

And what answer is given?

As we continue in our study of 2 Thessalonians 1:7, we discover when God will settle the score: "And he will give rest to you who are troubled and to us also when the Lord Jesus appears with burning fire from heaven with his powerful angels" (NCV).

When Christ returns, He will return in judgment!

STOP & PRAY

Ask God to help you remember that you never have to get even with someone who has hurt you. Thank Him for being in control.

SCOOP 4

Then he will punish those who do not know God and who do not obey the Good News about our Lord Jesus Christ. Those people will be punished with a destruction that continues forever. They will be kept away from the Lord and from his great power.
—*2 Thessalonians 1:8–9 NCV*

Christ said more about hell than anyone else. When Paul said, "Those people will be punished with a destruction that continues forever," he was talking about hell.

Hell is

_____ a. an eternity of chemistry homework.

_____ b. eternal separation from God and eternal pain.

_____ c. no TV, email, or communication with my friends.

_____ d. hard manual labor.

Unfortunately, many people have become so accustomed to hearing the word *hell* that it's thought of as a slang term instead of reality. The truth is, hell is real, and it's indescribably awful!

If you asked your non-Christian friends about hell, how would they respond? Do they even believe there *is* a hell?

Check this out: "I will show you the one to fear. Fear the one who has the power to kill you and also to throw you into hell. Yes, this is the one you should fear" (Luke 12:5 NCV).

Jesus is speaking in the above passage. By what He says, you can surmise that hell is

    ____ a. a fairy tale.

    ____ b. very real.

    ____ c. something that exists only in books.

    ____ d. a big shopping mall.

We don't hear a lot of preaching about hell, do we? We hear a lot about the positive things Jesus will do for us—that He'll forgive us, provide us with a purpose, give us joy, etc.—but we don't hear a lot about what He has saved us from: hell.

If you're a Christian, God has not only forgiven your sins, but He has saved you from hell! That's something to get excited about. Why do you think we don't talk much about hell?

STOP & PRAY ————————————————————————————————

Take a moment to write God a note in the space below and thank Him for saving you and giving you eternal life:

SCOOP 5

Those people will be punished with a destruction that continues forever. They will be kept away from the Lord and from his great power. This will happen on the day when the Lord Jesus comes to receive glory because of his holy people. And all the people who have believed will be amazed at Jesus. You will be in that group, because you believed what we told you.

—2 Thessalonians 1:9–10 NCV

Look specifically at the first part of this passage. Who will be punished with a destruction that continues forever and kept away from the Lord (mark all that apply)?

_____ a. Those who have not accepted Jesus Christ as their personal Savior.

_____ b. Those who don't obey the Lord.

_____ c. Those who haven't confessed that Jesus Christ is Lord.

Actually, all of the above describe those who will be punished eternally in hell. Many assume if they're good, try to do right, and believe in God, they'll end up in heaven. This is a false assumption. Believing in God isn't enough to save you. Even Satan believes in God!

But doesn't the Bible say that all who believe in Jesus will be saved? Yes it does. Let's read Romans 3:22: "God makes people right with himself through their faith in Jesus Christ. This is true for all who believe in Christ, because all people are the same" (NCV).

The Bible has been translated from the original Greek to many different languages. This is a good thing, because the more who can read God's Word, the better. But in the original language, the definition for the word we use as *believe* means "to completely adhere to." In other words, this passage is talking about those who surrender their lives to Christ . . . will be saved and will be made righteous.

That's a lot different from simply being a good person, isn't it? Good people who don't have a personal relationship with Christ will not enter the kingdom of heaven.

Grab your Bible and turn to John 14:6. Who is the way, the truth and the life?

According to this verse, how can someone approach God and enter heaven?

STOP & PRAY ───

End your quiet time by asking God to bring some people to your mind who might not know Him. (These can be people you know, or they may be people you only know about—such as public personalities or celebrities.) Pray for those He brings to your mind.

SCOOP 6

That is why we always pray for you, asking our God to help you live the kind of life he called you to live. We pray that with his power God will help you do the good things you want and perform the works that come from your faith.

—2 Thessalonians 1:11 NCV

If you're walking with Christ and have accepted Him as Lord of your life, God counts you worthy of His calling. No, you don't deserve it, but because Jesus saturates your life, God sees His Son when He looks at you.

How does this make you feel?

By His power, He can fulfill your desire to become all He wants you to be!

We pray all this so that the name of our Lord Jesus Christ will have glory in you, and you will have glory in him. That glory comes from the grace of our God and the Lord Jesus Christ.
—2 THESSALONIANS 1:12 NCV

When Christ returns, He will be glorified not only *among* you, but in you! How can Christ be glorified in you right now (circle all that apply)?

By the way I live

BY NOT DOING MY HOMEWORK

IN MY SINGING

In how I drive

In my reactions to those around me

WHAT I DO IN MY SPARE TIME

IN WHAT I WEAR

The jokes I tell

In athletics

My grades

Think of an older Christian whom you admire. How do you see Christ glorified in his or her life?

STOP & PRAY ———————————————————————————

Pray that God will glorify Himself through your life every day.

ACCOUNTABILITY

Way to go! You made it all the way through the first chapter of 2 Thessalonians. You're growing closer to Christ because you're taking His Word seriously. Now develop some accountability by grabbing a Christian pal (someone of the same sex) and discussing the following questions together. Strive for total honesty! Don't be defensive when your account-ability partner points out something in your life you need to work on. That's what accountability is all about.

* In the first part of this book, we talked about church. How has God been glorified in my life through my church attendance and involvement during the past few weeks?

* How have I demonstrated Christ's peace this past week?
* Have I encouraged someone by praying for him/her and affirming him/her this past week? If so, who? If not, why?
* Was there a time this past week when I tried to settle the score with someone who hurt me? How *should* I have responded?

✳ BRAIN SAVER!

Save the following verse in your brain by memorizing it with your friend. Say it to each other tomorrow over the phone or when you get together.

God will do what is right. He will give trouble to those who trouble you.
—2 THESSALONIANS 1:6 NCV

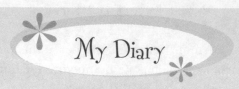

My Diary

This is your very own personal space. You can do whatever you want with it (make out an early Christmas list, file your algebra homework here, write your own mini-novel . . . whatever!), but try to always include the following:

- A list of stuff you need to pray about. (Later, as God answers them, go back and write in the date He answered each prayer.)
- Any verses we studied in the previous chapter that you don't get? Record them here and ask your Sunday school teacher, parents, youth leader, or pastor about them.
- Briefly summarize what you learned from studying this chapter.

My Diary

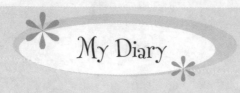

My Diary

CHAPTER TWO

Hope That Lasts Forever

SCOOP 1

Brothers and sisters, we have something to say about the coming of our Lord Jesus Christ and the time when we will meet together with him. Do not become easily upset in your thinking or afraid if you hear that the day of the Lord has already come. Someone may say this in a prophecy or in a message or in a letter as if it came from us.

—2 Thessalonians 2:1–2 NCV

"The time when we will meet together with him" is the rapture of the Christians. The Rapture is when

    ___ a. school is dismissed.

    ___ b. Christians will disappear from the earth in the twinkling of an eye and ascend to meet Christ in the air.

    ___ c. spring break happens.

    ___ d. we all eat a giant breakfast buffet in heaven.

"The day of the Lord" is a time of judgment on unbelievers. It marks the beginning of the Great Tribulation and continues through the Millennium. A false report was circulating among the believers in Thessalonica that the day of the Lord had already come.

Because many Christians were enduring persecution, it was easy for them to believe that they were in the midst of the Great Tribulation. Paul was setting the record straight by telling his confused Christian friends not to believe the rumors.

The Bible gives us specific things to look for that will happen before the day of the Lord. Grab your Bible and turn to Acts 2:20. According to this Scripture, what will happen to the sun?

What will happen to the moon?

Now flip to 2 Peter 3:10. How will the day of the Lord come?

The unbelievers will be caught off guard. They won't be expecting the Rapture, or Christ's return and judgment. As no one expects a thief in the middle of the night, non-Christians won't be expecting the last days.

According to 2 Peter 3:10, what will happen to the heavens?

What will be destroyed by fire?

Again, the day of the Lord isn't referring to the Christians. This is specifically for the unbelievers. Let's look at Revelation 6:15–17 (NIV):

> *Then the kings of the earth, the princes, the generals, the rich, the mighty, and every slave and every free man hid in caves and among the rocks of the mountains. They called to the mountains and the rocks, "Fall on us and hide us from the face of him who sits on the throne and from the wrath of the Lamb! For the great day of their wrath has come, and who can stand?"*

Christians won't be hiding from God. Christians can't wait to be with God. These verses say that the unbelievers will be afraid and will rather die than have to face God's judgment.

Are you where you need to be spiritually? Check out this verse: "God, examine me and know my heart; test me and know my nervous thoughts. See if there is any bad thing in me. Lead me on the road to everlasting life" (Psalm 139:23–24 NCV).

STOP & PRAY

Take a moment to rewrite these two verses as your own personal prayer, asking God to help you know for sure you're where you need to be spiritually:

SCOOP 2

Do not let anyone fool you in any way. That day of the Lord will not come until the turning away from God happens and the Man of Evil, who is on his way to hell, appears.

—2 Thessalonians 2:3 NCV

What does it mean "to fool" someone?

Describe a time when you were deceived:

Describe a time when you deceived someone else:

Paul told the Christians not to be fooled or deceived in any way. In fact, we're not to have anything to do with deceit! Grab your Bible and turn to 1 Peter 2:1. List the things we're supposed to rid ourselves of:

Now flip to 1 Peter 2:22. This passage describes Christ. What two things were not found in Him?

    1. _____

    2. _____

Check out this description of heaven: "Nothing unclean and no one who does shameful things or tells lies will ever go into it. Only those whose names are written in the Lamb's book of life will enter the city" (Revelation 21:27 NCV).

What are the characteristics of those who will not enter heaven?

Let's read 2 Thessalonians 2:3 again: "Do not let anyone fool you in any way. That day of the Lord will not come until the turning away from God happens and the Man of Evil, who is on his way to hell, appears" (NCV).

The Day of the Lord won't happen until two things occur:

#1: There will be a great rebellion (or falling away) in the world.

#2: The Antichrist will reveal himself.

Though we're seeing rebellion in the world right now, it will be greatly multiplied. Describe the rebellious acts you see in the world today:

STOP & PRAY

Ask God to help you refrain from being rebellious—toward Him and toward others in authority over you. Tell Him you want to grow in your desire to follow and obey Him in every area of your life.

SCOOP 3

He will be against and put himself above anything called God or anything that people worship. And that Man of Evil will even go into God's Temple and sit there and say that he is God.

—2 Thessalonians 2:4 NCV

The Antichrist will claim he is God, and many will believe him. He will perform miracles, but they'll be done with Satan's power. The Antichrist will be filled with Satan. In other words, Satan will pour himself into a living human vessel.

During the first few years of the Tribulation, the Antichrist will proclaim world peace and people will readily accept him as a world leader.

He'll not only proclaim world peace, but he'll make it happen! Revelation chapter 13 portrays the Antichrist as a beast coming out of the sea who is given great power. Some believe he'll bring Western Europe together and will provide a peaceful solution between Jews and Muslims.

People will watch him in awe and say, "Wow! This guy is our hero. He's fantastic. He can do anything!"

Listen to what God says about this person:

I told you when I was with you that all this would happen. Do you not remember? And now you know what is stopping that Man of Evil so he will appear at the right time. (2 Thessalonians 2:5–6 NCV)

God is always in control! When you hear about earthquakes, hurricanes, famine, and other catastrophic disasters, you may be tempted to think God has lost control. But He hasn't!

God is not surprised by anything. He doesn't pace heaven wringing His hands, saying, "Now what do I do?"

And God knows every detail concerning the end of the world. The Antichrist hasn't revealed himself yet, because God hasn't allowed that to happen. But there will come a time when God will remove His Holy Spirit, permitting evil to run rampant across the world as we've never experienced.

The secret power of evil is already working in the world, but there is one who is stopping that power. And he will continue to stop it until he is taken out of the way.
—2 THESSALONIANS 2:7 NCV

It is obvious Satan is at work in our world. List five ways you see evidence of his influence in the world:

1. _____

2. _____

3. _____

4. _____

5. _____

List three ways Satan tries to influence you personally:

1. _____

2. _____

3. _____

STOP & PRAY

Close your devotional time by asking God to help you become a person of integrity. Ask for His help to never purposely deceive anyone again.

SCOOP 4

When God removes the Holy Spirit from the earth and allows Satan to live out his lawlessness, it'll be like opening a bottle of soda pop that's been shaken. Evil will spew forth in great power and with immeasurable speed. God will allow Satan to have his "day." (But it will be only temporary!)

Then that Man of Evil will appear, and the Lord Jesus will kill him with the breath that comes from his mouth and will destroy him with the glory of his coming.

—2 Thessalonians 2:8 NCV

This "Man of Evil"—the Antichrist—will appear to be unstoppable. He'll control the entire world, and no military or any other world power will be able to thwart his plans. The only power that can stop the Antichrist is Christ Himself. Christ's coming will finally end the power of Satan and the work of the Antichrist.

According to 2 Thessalonians 2:8, how will Jesus overthrow the Antichrist?

Grab your Bible and turn to Genesis 1:3. How did God create light?

Now read Genesis 1:6–8. How did God create the sky?

Check out Genesis 1:9–10. How did God create dry land?

All God had to do to create the world was to simply
    ____ a. complete a course called "World Creating 101."
    ____ b. mix a little of this and a little of that.
    ____ c. speak it into existence.
    ____ d. follow an instruction manual.

Just as God created the entire world by His words, He will defeat sin with one breath. Take another peek at 2 Thessalonians 2:8. Who will be destroyed by the glory of Christ's coming?

STOP & PRAY

End your quiet time by asking God to help you resist Satan's influence in your life. Meditate on 1 Corinthians 10:13.

SCOOP 5

The Man of Evil will come by the power of Satan. He will have great power, and he will do many different false miracles, signs, and wonders. He will use every kind of evil to trick those who are lost. They will die, because they refused to love the truth. (If they loved the truth, they would be saved.)
—2 Thessalonians 2:9–10 NCV

People sometimes make the mistake of believing every miracle they witness is of God. Though God is all-powerful and has victory over Satan, Satan still has a great amount of power. He has the ability to perform miracles, possess people's minds and bodies, and speak through human voices. Don't make the mistake of assuming all miracles are of God; they're not!

Describe a time when you mistook something as being real when it was actually a fake:

Let's look at 2 Thessalonians 2:10 again: "They will die, because they refused to love the truth" (NCV).

God will save anyone who confesses his or her sins, accepts Christ as Savior, and lives in obedience to Him. Check this out: "God makes people right with himself through their faith in Jesus Christ. This is true for all who believe in Christ, because all people are the same" (Romans 3:22 NCV).

According to this passage, who can be saved?

In the original language in which the Bible was written, the word *believe* meant much more than "head knowledge." Simply believing in God with your mind isn't enough to make you a Christian. Even Satan believes in God.

"To believe in" meant to adhere your life to; commit 100 percent to. That, of course, involves your heart, your actions, and your lifestyle.

Grab your Bible and flip to Romans 3:23–24. Copy this passage in the space below.

According to the above Scripture, who has sinned?

Now turn to John 14:6. Who is the way?

Who is the truth?

Who is the life?

According to this passage, how many paths lead to heaven?

   ___ a. Too many to count.

   ___ b. Any good religion will lead to heaven.

   ___ c. There's only one way to heaven, and it's through a relation-ship with Jesus Christ.

   ___ d. Going to a church, temple, or synagogue on a regular basis.

STOP & PRAY

Ask God to help you share His truth with those around you.

ACCOUNTABILITY

Way to go! You made it halfway through the second chapter of 2 Thessalonians. You're growing closer to Christ because you're taking His Word seriously. Now get with your accountability partner and discuss the following questions together. Strive for total honesty! Remember . . . don't be defensive when your accountability partner points out something in your life you need to work on. That's what accountability is all about.

   ✳ Have I been deceived this week? Have I been deceptive with someone else this week?

✳ Antichrist is a person, but we can be "anti" (against) Christ in specific areas of our lives. *Anti* not only means "against," but it means "taking the place of." Is there an area in my life in which I struggle with something or someone taking the place of Christ?

✳ Describe a time I stood firm in my faith this week.

✳ How have you seen me "live out" my salvation this week?

✳ How have I encouraged others this week?

✳ BRAIN SAVER!

Save the following verse in your brain by memorizing it with your friend. Say it to each other tomorrow over the phone or when you get together.

So all those will be judged guilty who did not believe the truth, but enjoyed doing evil.
—2 THESSALONIANS 2:12 NCV

My Diary

My Diary

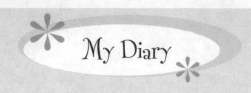

My Diary

CHAPTER THREE

Stand Firm

Let's take another glance at 2 Thessalonians 2:10 (NCV): "They will die, because they refused to love the truth."

According to the above verse, who will not be saved?

In this particular passage, "love the truth" can be paralleled to "believe the truth." What happens to those who refuse to believe the truth?

People often assume that good people will go to heaven. "But she's such a wonderful person," someone will say. Or, "He does so much for others."

Our good works will not get us to heaven! The only thing that guarantees us entrance into God's perfect kingdom is His grace and a relationship with Him.

Read what the Bible has to say about this: "You have been saved by grace through believing. You did not save yourselves; it was a gift from God. It was not the result of your own efforts, so you cannot brag about it " (Ephesians 2:8–9).

What two things listed above are ingredients to your salvation?

1. _____

2. _____

Do you know some good people who don't have a personal relationship with Christ? List a few of their names and ask God to give you opportunity to share the gospel with them. Pray for them consistently.

1. _____

2. _____

3. _____

For this reason God sends them something powerful that leads them away from the truth so they will believe a lie. So all those will be judged guilty who did not believe the truth, but enjoyed doing evil.

—2 THESSALONIANS 2:11–12 NCV

God will allow those who aren't saved to believe the lies of the Antichrist. Lots of people today have heard the gospel but refuse to believe it. Second Thessalonians 2:11–12 tells us that God will send a strong delusion to them. God has graciously given them ample opportunity to accept His truth, but they still refuse. These are the people who will openly accept lies and deceptions.

STOP & PRAY

Pray that God will continue to tenderize your heart and keep you open to His teaching. Ask Him to bless you with discernment and wisdom so you can differentiate truth from lies.

SCOOP 2

Brothers and sisters, whom the Lord loves, God chose you from the beginning to be saved. So we must always thank God for you. You are saved by the Spirit that makes you holy and by your faith in the truth.

—2 Thessalonians 2:13 NCV

Grab your Bible and turn to 2 Thessalonians 1:3. What similarities do you see in this verse and in 2 Thessalonians 2:13?

Check out 2 Peter 3:9. According to this verse, it's clearly God's will that everyone be saved! He doesn't want anyone to perish. Christ's timing is perfect. He won't haphazardly return to earth during a slow day in heaven. He has perfectly timed His return! Why doesn't He come back right now? He's graciously giving us more time to spread the gospel so more will be saved.

Flip to Matthew 24:14. According to this Scripture, when will the end come?

Paul mentions the "sanctifying work of the Spirit." *Sanctification* is the process of becoming one with Christ. It involves total surrender and a commitment to holy living. Sanctification means to be set apart for sacred use.

Get your Bible and turn to Romans 15:16 (NIV). According to this verse, who sanctifies us?

    ___ a. Our pastor

    ___ b. Our parents

    ___ c. The Holy Spirit

    ___ d. Our church

Now check out 1 Corinthians 6:11 (NIV). This verse describes sanctification as not only being set apart for sacred use but also as

    ___ a. a deep internal spiritual cleansing.

    ___ b. something that happens only in adults.

    ___ c. something you can get only at church camp.

Let's look at Paul's first letter to the Thessalonians. He addresses sanctification in 5:23: "Now may God himself, the God of peace, make you pure, belonging only to him May your whole self—spirit, soul, and body—be kept safe and without fault when our Lord Jesus Christ comes" (NCV).

The above Scripture leads you to believe that sanctification is

    ___ a. something that's wishy-washy.

    ___ b. only done in your heart.

    ___ c. very thorough and deep.

    ___ d. only done in your mind.

Sanctification affects your entire life! The Holy Spirit wants to saturate you. He doesn't want to simply live in your heart; He wants to take up residence in your mind, too. He wants to guide your thinking and affect your actions and reactions. He wants to sanctify you thoroughly, wholly, and deeply.

STOP & PRAY ───────────────────────────────

If you've never made a commitment of total surrender to the lordship of Christ, tell Him you want to do that right now. Ask Him to take charge of your life, and tell Him you're relinquishing your rights to His authority.

SCOOP 3

God used the Good News that we preached to call you to be saved so you can share in the glory of our Lord Jesus Christ.

—*2 Thessalonians 2:14 NCV*

There's a big difference between living close to Christ and living inside Him. Paul says that God wants you to "share in the glory of our Lord Jesus Christ." In other words, through the power of His Holy Spirit—in the process of sanctification—God calls you to become one with His Son. This requires total surrender.

List two things you've struggled with that make it difficult for you to become one with Christ:

1. _____

2. _____

Will you give those areas of your life to God right now? Becoming one with Christ requires totally yielding to His authority.

In the space below, write out a prayer giving God absolute charge of every single area of your life. Ask Him to sanctify you wholly and to cleanse you deep within. Tell Him you want the power of His Spirit released within you. Start living in this power!

So, brothers and sisters, stand strong and continue to believe the teachings we gave you in our speaking and in our letter.
—2 THESSALONIANS 2:15 NCV

Paul reminded the believers to remember and to put into practice the things he had taught them. It's important not to forget what we've learned from the Bible. The Word of God provides strength to Christians. Without His truth, we wouldn't stand very tall or for very long.

Read how Paul described the Word of God in 2 Timothy 3:16–17: "The whole Bible was given to us by inspiration from God and is useful to teach us what is true and to make us realize what is wrong in our lives; it straightens us out and helps us do what is right. It is God's way of making us well prepared at every point, fully equipped to do good to everyone" (TLB).

According to the above verses, how was the Bible given to us?

What does God's Word teach us?

What does the Bible help us do?

What does God use to make us well-prepared?

Not only is the Bible our road map for life; it's also our spiritual heritage. We can learn from the saints who have lived before us and put biblical principles into practice.

Grab your Bible and turn to Hebrews 12:1 (NIV). Who surrounds us and cheers us onward to spiritual victory?

Take a moment to describe your personal spiritual heritage. (Are your parents Christians? Your grandparents? When did you become a Christian? What's your spiritual history?)

STOP & PRAY ———————————————————————————

Ask God to help you continue to make devotions (your quiet time with Him and your Bible reading and Bible study) a consistent part of your life after you've finished this book.

SCOOP 4

May our Lord Jesus Christ himself and God our Father encourage you and strengthen you in every good thing you do and say. God loved us, and through his grace he gave us a good hope and encouragement that continues forever.
—2 Thessalonians 2:16–17 NCV

What is "grace" in this verse?

____ a. A senior citizen who goes to my church

____ b. Having a school assembly during the same time the big chemistry test was scheduled

____ c. A new board game by Milton Bradley

____ d. Receiving undeserved favor

According to the above Scripture, who loves you?

How does He want you to approach carrying out good deeds and words?

God is faithful! He doesn't command you to do something and then tell you He'll check up on you at the same time next year. Turn to Hebrews 13:5. Inserting your own name, write a note to yourself from God based on this Scripture:

Take another look at 2 Thessalonians 2:16–17. How long does God want to encourage you?

Describe a specific time when God encouraged you through another Christian:

Describe a specific time when you were encouraged by God's Word. Do you remember which Scripture encouraged you?

When things aren't going your way, allow God to turn your discouragement into encouragement. How? (1) By thanking Him for His faithfulness; (2) by committing your situation to Him; (3) by counting your blessings.

We don't focus enough on God's blessings. Take a moment to list some of the blessings God has given you:

1. _____

2. _____

3. _____

4. _____

5. _____

6. _____

7. _____

8. _____

9. _____

10. _____

STOP & PRAY ————————————————————————————

Ask God to help you become acutely aware of His blessings in your life. Tell Him you don't want to take His goodness for granted.

ACCOUNTABILITY

Way to go! You made it all the way through the second chapter of 2 Thessalonians. You're growing closer to Christ because you're taking His Word seriously. Now get with your accountability partner and discuss the following questions together. Strive for total honesty! Remember . . . don't be defensive when your accountability partner points out something in your life you need to work on. That's what accountability is all about.

* Sanctification is the process of becoming one with Christ; becoming holy; being set apart. How have I demonstrated that growth in my spiritual life this week?
* How have you seen the biblical teachings I've been taught reflected in my life this week?

* Do I thank God for influential people in my life? If so, whom do you hear me thanking Him for? If not, will you hold me account-able for thanking Him consistently for these special people?
* Have you noticed any area in my life that I haven't lived with integrity and truth this week?

✳ BRAIN SAVER!

Save the following verse in your brain by memorizing it with your friend. Say it to each other tomorrow over the phone or when you get together.

Brothers and sisters, whom the Lord loves, God chose you from the beginning to be saved. So we must always thank God for you. You are saved by the Spirit that makes you holy and by your faith in the truth.
　　　　　—2 THESSALONIANS 2:13 NCV

My Diary

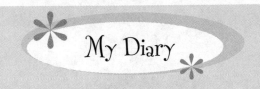

My Diary

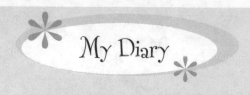

My Diary

CHAPTER FOUR

Lazybones

SCOOP 1

And now, brothers and sisters, pray for us that the Lord's teaching will continue to spread quickly and that people will give honor to that teaching, just as happened with you.

—2 Thessalonians 3:1 NCV

As Christians, we have a responsibility to pray for one another. As Paul began the final chapter in his second letter to the Thessalonians, he reminded them that their prayers were needed.

What specifically does Paul ask his friends to pray for?

Whom do you regularly pray for?

What situations do you regularly pray for?

Flip back to 2 Thessalonians 1:11. Paul reminded his friends that he was constantly praying for them. What did he pray?

Now grab your Bible and go back to 1 Thessalonians 5:17. What did Paul tell the Christians to do continually?

Read James 5:13. What should we do when we're in trouble?

Check out 1 Peter 4:7: "The time is near when all things will end. So think clearly and control yourselves so you will be able to pray" (NCV).

What two ingredients listed above are helpful to someone's prayer life?

1. _____

2. _____

Grab your Bible and turn to Jeremiah 29:12. What will God do when you pray?

Turn to Jeremiah 42:3. For what two things did the people ask the prophet Jeremiah to pray?

1. _____

2. _____

You can actually pray about (circle all that apply):

Grades   Your shoes
           ANYTHING
                                        Stress
    Dating   Praises
              Teachers   **WEATHER**
Your future spouse
              JOB
                      BLESSINGS
    Headaches
              Parents   THE PROM
Travel
            Your career   MONEY
    Everything
                      Bitterness
ANGER
                          WHAT TO EAT FOR LUNCH
            SICKNESS
    Pets   Friends

There's nothing too big or too small to pray about! If it concerns you, it concerns your heavenly Father. What does Luke 12:7 tell us that God knows about?

If God knows and is concerned about that, He's certainly concerned about everything else in your life! Your prayers make a difference.

STOP & PRAY

Make time daily to pray for your own needs and for others. Stop right now and pray about anything that's on your heart.

SCOOP 2

*And pray that we will be protected from stubborn
and evil people, because not all people believe.*
—*2 Thessalonians 3:2 NCV*

You may recall in the introduction to this study, Paul was run out of Thessalonica and persecuted by wicked men. In the verse above, he was asking the Thessalonians to pray for his deliverance from evil people who didn't share a personal faith in Christ.

Again, Christians have a responsibility to pray for one another. Think about it: You have a direct line to the King of kings! Why wouldn't you want to tap into that line and use it?!

These wicked men are also mentioned by Paul in Acts 17:5–7. According to these verses, the wicked men accused Paul and his followers of

____ a. defying Caesar's decrees.

____ b. driving their chariots on the wrong side of the street.

____ c. riding donkeys over the speed limit on the highway.

Paul did preach that there was another King besides Caesar. Who was the King about whom Paul preached?

____ a. King Wenceslaus

____ b. King Charles

____ c. King Jesus Christ

____ d. Henry VIII

Though Paul openly preached about Christ, he also taught how we should respond to those in authority over us. Grab your Bible and read Romans 13:1. According to this verse, how should we respond to those in authority?

The wicked men from whom Paul wanted deliverance were not only persecuting him physically, but they were also lying about him. Describe a time when someone said something untrue about you. How did it make you feel? How did you resolve the issue?

We need to remember that Christians in many countries are currently being persecuted for their faith. You may be tempted to think it's useless to pray for people far away and for those you don't even know. But your prayers for others really do make a difference. Take a moment to write a prayer for persecuted believers:

But the Lord is faithful and will give you strength and will protect you from the Evil One.

—2 Thessalonians 3:3 NCV

According to the above passage, what two things will God provide for you?

____ a. Joy and laughter

____ b. Strength and protection

____ c. Money and new clothes

____ d. Housing and cars

God is faithful! Though we often let Him down, He never lets us down. God gives Christians two promises in Hebrews 13:5. What are they?

1. _____

2. _____

What promise is given in Matthew 28:20?

According to Jude 24 (NIV), we can count on God's faithfulness to keep us from what?

Based on Philippians 1:6, what will God continue and finish in your life?

Turn to 2 Corinthians 1:3–4. What does God promise to do when you're experiencing trouble?

He does this so you can do what for others?

___ a. Ignore them.

___ b. Comfort them.

___ c. Sing about them.

___ d. Play soccer with them.

Grab your Bible and read 1 Corinthians 10:13. What can you trust God to do for you when you are tempted?

And when you are tempted, God will always provide

___ a. a friend to turn to.

___ b. homework to distract you.

___ c. a nearby shopping mall.

___ d. a way out.

STOP & PRAY ────────────────────────────────

Close your devotional time by asking God to help you give Him your temptations as soon as you're faced with them!

SCOOP 3

The Lord makes us feel sure that you are doing and will continue to do the things we told you. May the Lord lead your hearts into God's love and Christ's patience.

—2 Thessalonians 3:4–5 NCV

It's important that Christians obey God. Jesus said in John 14:15 that if we love Him we will

____ a. put more money in the offering plate at church.

____ b. obey Him.

____ c. wear a sign that reads "God Is Love!"

____ d. bake cookies for the homeless.

Paul's teaching was directly from God, so he was reminding the Thessalonians to obey his teaching. He had confidence in the Thessalonian church and affirmed their devotion to Christ.

How do those around you know that you're devoted to Jesus Christ?

Brothers and sisters, by the authority of our Lord Jesus Christ we command you to stay away from any believer who refuses to work and does not follow the teaching we gave you.
—2 THESSALONIANS 3:6 NCV

In this verse, Paul gave us a
___ a. suggestion.
___ b. good idea.
___ c. command.
___ d. piece of advice.

It's one thing to witness to nonbelievers. Jesus told us to go into all the world and share the gospel with everyone (Matthew 28:19), but many take this as an excuse to establish close friendships with people who don't have a personal relationship with Christ.

How can you befriend nonbelievers without starting to live like them?

Check out Romans 12:2: "Do not change yourselves to be like the people of this world, but be changed within by a new way of thinking. Then you will be able to decide what God wants for you; you will know what is good and pleasing to him and what is perfect" (NCV).

God calls His children to become

    ___ a. conformed.

    ___ b. transformed.

    ___ c. deformed.

    ___ d. reformed.

According to Romans 12:2, what will you be able to do once you allow God to transform and renew your mind?

STOP & PRAY

Close your devotional time by telling God you want Him to rid you of anything and everything that prevents others from seeing Him in your life. Ask Him to bring those specific things to your mind; then commit them to Him.

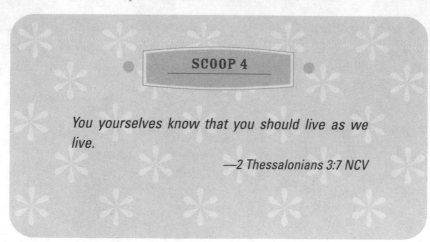

SCOOP 4

You yourselves know that you should live as we live.

—*2 Thessalonians 3:7 NCV*

Paul lived in consistent obedience to the lordship of Jesus Christ. He was so in tune with Christ that he felt confident enough to tell other Christians to follow his example.

Are you obeying Christ in such a way that you can easily say to those around you, "Copy my lifestyle"?

If not, what would need to change in order for you to truthfully say that to people?

We were not lazy when we were with you. And when we ate another person's food, we always paid for it. We worked very hard night and day so we would not be an expense to any of you.

—2 THESSALONIANS 3:7–8 NCV

Paul was a man of integrity. He never took advantage of those to whom he preached. In fact, he didn't even charge them for his services. He supported himself through a life of making tents (Acts 18:3).

He didn't have a hotel reservation when he arrived in a town to share the gospel. Paul didn't receive a love offering on his initial visit to a city. He never wanted new Christians to think he was sharing God's news for money. Paul mentioned this not only in 2 Thessalonians, but he also mentioned it in his letters to the Christians in Corinth.

Once the churches were established and Paul made return visits to them, he did receive an offering. In his letter to the Philippians, Paul thanked them for their gift. He told the Galatians they should give. Paul wanted God's people to learn how to care for those who traveled and shared the gospel, but he was also extremely careful never to take advantage of Christians or to use the gospel for selfish means. This also enabled him to tell others to copy his behavior. He was careful to set a godly example.

Describe someone you know who lives a godly life of integrity. What specific things set him or her apart from everyone else?

STOP & PRAY

Close your devotional time by asking God to help you become a disciple of integrity. Ask Him to show you anything in your life that's not consistent with integrity. Be willing to seek forgiveness for that area and give it to Him.

ACCOUNTABILITY

Way to go! You made it halfway through the third chapter of 2 Thessalonians. You're growing closer to Christ because you're taking His Word seriously. Now get with your accountability partner and discuss the following questions together. Strive for total honesty! Remember . . . don't be defensive when your accountability partner points out something in your life you need to work on. That's what accountability is all about.

* Have I prayed effectively and consistently for others this week? Have I kept my word when I've told people I'd pray for them?
* Was there a time this week that I was a busybody or a trouble-maker? Have I gossiped about someone? Have I worked to further God's kingdom by loving others or giving to them in specific ways?
* Have I consistently prayed for others this week? Ask me whom I've prayed for.
* Have I hung out with anyone I shouldn't have this past week? Have I been influenced by the wrong people?

*BRAIN SAVER!

Save the following verse in your brain by memorizing it with your friend. Say it to each other tomorrow over the phone or when you get together.

May the Lord lead your hearts into God's love and Christ's patience.
                        —2 THESSALONIANS 3:5 NCV

My Diary

My Diary

My Diary

Work Smart; Live Smart

We had the right to ask you to help us, but we worked to take care of ourselves so we would be an example for you to follow.

—*2 Thessalonians 3:9 NCV*

In this verse, Paul was explaining to the Thessalonians that since he led them to the Lord and established their church, he had a right to expect an offering. He chose not to ask for an offering, however, because the Christians were new in their faith, and Paul didn't want to confuse them.

Why might asking for money have confused the Thessalonians?

Above all else, Paul wanted to be a holy example. What actions in your life are an example of holiness for others to follow?

When we were with you, we gave you this rule: "Anyone who refuses to work should not eat." (2 Thessalonians 3:10 NCV)

Notice that Paul didn't mention those who *can't* work. He talked about those who *refused* to work. The Bible is clear that Christians should show compassion for those who are needy and can't work.

But there were a few fanatics in Thessalonica who had taken Paul's last letter to their church to an extreme. Since Paul had told them that Christ could return at any time, they stopped working. They simply thought, *Well, Christ is going to return, so why work? Let's just wait for Him!*

Christ was radical and fervent and outspoken, but He wasn't fanatical. He was practical. If He had been a fanatic, He may have said, "It's not important for Me to work in the carpenter's shop; I'm going to be crucified anyway." Or "Why go to church? I know who I am."

Yes, God wants us to live expectantly of Christ's return, but not so much so that our noses are pressed against the window and we cease to live practical lives. Even though we know He will return one day, we should continue to study, work, prepare, and live our lives in a way that pleases Him.

Is there an area of your life in which you tend to be fanatical? If so, explain. Place that area under God's control and ask Him to help you be more practical.

STOP & PRAY ───────────────────────────────

Ask God to help you live expectantly but practically. Ask Him to point out any area of your life in which you're too fanatical. Give that area to Him.

SCOOP 2

We hear that some people in your group refuse to work. They do nothing but busy themselves in other people's lives.

—*2 Thessalonians 3:11 NCV*

What's a "busybody"?

____ a. Someone who works really hard

____ b. Someone who's always trying to figure out other people's business and get in the middle of things that don't pertain to him

____ c. Someone who always has too much homework

____ d. Someone who travels a lot

Paul let us in on what was happening in the Thessalonian church. We learn that some of the Christians weren't working to earn a living. Paul told us in the next verse that we need to earn the bread we eat. This particular little group of people weren't doing anything constructive. They were busy; but they weren't busy in a good way. They were simply busybodies. They got in the way of those who were truly working at doing what was right. They were nuisances.

Sometimes we have to take a few steps back from people who aren't enhancing our walk with Christ. Perhaps you have some Christian friends who are negative, or cause you to question your faith, or complain about the way the youth group is run.

They're not enhancing your faith. They're not helping you draw closer to the Lord. It's okay for you to distance yourself from people like that. Don't ignore them, but don't feel you have to be an intimate friend. Choose to surround yourself with people who are positive, who encourage you in your faith, and who share your enthusiasm for God.

Describe a specific person in your life who *does* encourage you and support your relationship with Christ. How does that make you feel?

We command those people and beg them in the Lord Jesus Christ to work quietly and earn their own food.
　　　　　　　　　—2 Thessalonians 3:12 NCV

This is good practical advice from the apostle Paul. A lot of churches would be much healthier if the troublemakers (or busybodies) would settle down and concentrate on doing something constructive.

But you, brothers and sisters, never become tired of doing good.
　　　　　　　　　—2 Thessalonians 3:13 NCV

Do you ever get tired of doing the right thing? Take encouragement from this Scripture! No good thing goes unnoticed. God sees all that you do, and He will reward you in His time.

Let's take a peek at another letter Paul wrote. Grab your Bible and turn to Galatians 6:9. What did Paul encourage you *not* to do?

And what is the reward for those who don't give up?

STOP & PRAY ———————————————————————————————

Close your devotional time by asking God to help you encourage those around you. Pledge to make a call, send an e-mail, or mail a card to encourage someone today.

SCOOP 3

If some people do not obey what we tell you in this letter, then take note of them. Have nothing to do with them so they will feel ashamed. But do not treat them as enemies. Warn them as fellow believers.

—2 Thessalonians 3:14–15 NCV

Paul again advised us on how to react to troublemakers in the church. What did he tell us to do?

If one of your friends is gossiping about someone to you, it's probably safe to assume that she's also gossiping about you to someone else! Distance yourself from troublemakers. But Paul didn't tell you to be mean to these people. How are you told to approach a troublemaker who calls herself a Christian?

Now may the Lord of peace give you peace at all times and in every way. The Lord be with all of you.
                                        —2 THESSALONIANS 3:16 NCV

What did Paul want these Christians to experience from God?

What a comforting blessing Paul left with his readers as he wrapped up his letter. Is there someone you need to comfort? How can you comfort him or her?

According to 2 Thessalonians 3:16, how often should we experience God's peace?

_____ a. Once a week at church

_____ b. When we've aced a test at school

_____ c. At Christmas

_____ d. All the time

Check out Numbers 6:26. What will God give you when you turn your face toward Him?

According to Psalm 29:11, with what does God bless His people?

Read Psalm 34:14 (NIV). What are you to turn away from? And what are you to seek?

Proverbs 12:20 (NIV) says those who promote peace will receive something special. What is it?

Soak in John 14:27. What gift did Jesus say He would leave us?

STOP & PRAY ────────────────────────────

Is there something in your life that you don't have peace about? Write out a prayer concerning this specific area:

SCOOP 4

I, Paul, end this letter now in my own handwriting. All my letters have this to show they are from me. This is the way I write.
—*2 Thessalonians 3:17 NCV*

Paul signed this letter himself. He wanted to make sure his readers knew it was not a forgery.

The grace of our Lord Jesus Christ be with you all.
—2 THESSALONIANS 3:18 NCV)

Paul ended the letter to his Thessalonian friends the same way he started it. Flip back to 2 Thessalonians 1:2 and write down the gifts Paul wanted to leave with his readers:

Grab your Bible and turn to Romans 3:23–24 (NIV). We are justified freely by what?

Tune in to 2 Corinthians 6:1 (NIV). What must we be careful not to receive in vain?

According to Ephesians 1:7–8 (NIV), what has God lavished upon us?

Read Ephesians 4:7 and write below what each of us is given:

Now turn to 2 Peter 3:18 and list the two things in which we're instructed to grow:

    1. _____

    2. _____

According to Proverbs 3:34, who will receive grace?

Using the space below, paraphrase Proverbs 3:34:

Without God's grace, we'd be eternally lost. He didn't have to save us, forgive us, redeem us, or prepare an eternal home for us. It's only because of God's grace that we receive undeserved favor, forgiveness, and entrance into His perfect kingdom of heaven. That's worth getting excited about!

STOP & PRAY

Take a moment to write God a note in the space provided below, thanking Him for granting you grace though you don't deserve it:

ACCOUNTABILITY

Way to go! You just finished the third chapter of 2 Thessalonians. You're growing closer to Christ because you're taking His Word seriously. Now get with your accountability partner and discuss the following questions together. Strive for total honesty! Remember . . . don't be defensive when your accountability partner points out something in your life you need to work on. That's what accountability is all about.

* In what ways have I experienced God's peace this week?
* Describe a specific time I helped promote peace—a time I was a peacemaker.
* Can you help me identify any areas of idleness in my life?
* Do I consistently demonstrate God's grace in my own life and toward others?

✳ BRAIN SAVER!

Save the following verse in your brain by memorizing it with your friend. Say it to each other tomorrow over the phone or when you get together.

Now may the Lord of peace give you peace at all times and in every way.
—2 THESSALONIANS 3:16 NCV

My Diary

My Diary

My Diary

Wrapping it Up

There were rumors circulating in the Thessalonian church that Christ had already returned to earth and the Christians had been left behind. They felt hopeless.

Have you ever had to battle rumors? If someone has spread a rumor about you, you can understand how devastating it can be. It's easy to feel as though you have no hope.

But in this letter Paul assured the Thessalonian Christians that they *hadn't* missed Christ's return, and they had everything in the world to look forward to! When they realized that truth, the darkness lifted from their lives, and the sun began to shine in their hearts once again.

If you're living in expectancy of Christ's return . . . if you're allowing Him to develop integrity in you, your lifestyle will reflect Christ to others! Keep living for Christ and be encouraged by the eternal hope He has placed within you.

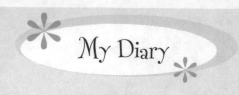

My Diary

My Diary

My Diary

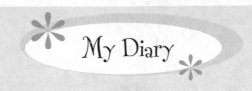

My Diary

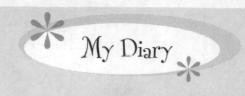

My Diary

Coming soon from

SUSIE SHELLENBERGER!